PEACOCK
DESIGNS
COLORING BOOK

MARTY NOBLE

DOVER PUBLICATIONS, INC.
MINEOLA, NEW YORK

NOTE

Easily recognizable by its elaborate, vibrantly colored tail feathers, the peacock ranks among the most beautiful creatures of the animal kingdom. As such, a coloring collection with this magnificent creature as its central motif will provide colorists with a broad array of detailed, imaginative designs. Part of Dover Publications' *Creative Haven* series, this book was created with the experienced colorist in mind. Meticulously rendered images of these fancy feathered friends set amongst exquisitely detailed backgrounds, provide each colorist with ample opportunity for experimentation with color, media, or technique. Plus, the perforated pages make displaying your finished work easy.

Copyright
Copyright © 2014 by Dover Publications, Inc.
All rights reserved.

Bibliographical Note
Peacock Designs Coloring Book is a new work, first published by Dover Publications, Inc., in 2014.

International Standard Book Number
ISBN-13: 978-0-486-77996-6
ISBN-10: 0-486-77996-3

Manufactured in the United States by Courier Corporation
77996306   2014
www.doverpublications.com